In the Cathedral
of My Undoing

In the Cathedral of My Undoing

Poems

Kellam Ayres

Gunpowder Press • Santa Barbara
2024

Published by Gunpowder Press
David Starkey, Editor
PO Box 60035
Santa Barbara, CA 93160-0035

Cover image: Corey Hendrickson

ISBN-13: 978-1-957062-11-2

www.gunpowderpress.com

For my family and my teachers

CONTENTS

I.

II.

III.

I think of the marvel of lust
Which can always, at any moment,
Become more than it believed,
And almost always is less

—James Dickey, "In the Lupanar at
Pompeii"

I.

The Haunting

In our village, the night sky flashes
with light, a storm of cloud, and at home,
phone sex between neighbors.
They text one-handed, their silent mouths
open and close to suggest longing,
or agony, or disbelief. Pleasure,
they've learned, has many masks.

Outside, a harvester fires up before dawn.
A tractor stands ready to spread manure.
What the woman said about her body,
what the man said is so hard—
words have taken them beyond the boundaries
of home, beyond the children and orchard
and greenhouse, the hen house—
an astonishing, impermanent relief—
words rising above the sweet loam,
the damp earth bathed in shit, crossed endlessly
by backhoe and mower, milk truck and draft horse.
Teenagers with buckets of feed before school,
texting too, to their friends, before hopping the bus.

We think they are still beautiful, our young,
we're convinced their virtue
does not dissolve each day—
but they've studied us, and so, already,
are caught by an ache that will linger for years.
And we think how hard it is to sustain this land,
this living, to keep on living—
how closely we toe ruin each day.

Ritual

A young couple fights in the street.
Her name is April. She is drunk and sad.
So is her boyfriend. He shouts her name

and follows her across the street,
but she doesn't respond. She sits on a bench
next to a fountain that hasn't worked in years.

Ten years spent looking down on Merchants Row,
its silent fountain and bench. Only the voices change.
Sometimes the man doesn't chase after the woman.

Sometimes he drives off. Sometimes he shoves her
and she hits him back. Sometimes he cries,
or they both cry, and it's pathetic—

the sound of two people crying in the street.
We know these sounds, don't we? Old love.
No good words for it. Sadness can't even

come close. Living above a bar and hearing
the end of one coupling after another.
It becomes you. Sometimes the man bends

at the waist with his hands in his hair. Sometimes
the woman won't stop screaming.
Sometimes they leave the bar and without touching

walk home. Years to learn the ways goodness
drains out of people. Outside the window
there is nothing to see now, only the dark reflection

of a figure looking down. Here comes a truck
making a delivery, idling before dawn. It's the start
of a new day. What about it can possibly be new?

Solving the Boulder Problem

I placed my left hand on a crimp, my right
on a side pull, tugged until I felt secure—
then, one at a time, my feet left the ground.

All winter I'd worked my fingers
raw at the gym, harnessed to a wall,
picking my way up the colorful holds.

But out here, near Abbey Pond,
on a fifteen-foot-high boulder
called The Rotten and the Wicked,

no ropes, no hot pink holds or tape
pointing the right way. Just a giant rock
with a crack running east-west.

My hands pressed the cold surface,
the rough, pale lichen. It seemed so intimate.
I wanted to apologize, somehow, say

I'm sorry to disturb, but I need to push
my body against you until I shake.
At eight I learned pleasure by climbing

a basketball pole, my legs wrapped tight
against the metal, then a shock of surprise—
I held on, and everything changed.

I approached the boulder again and again,
drenched from the effort, red-cheeked,
every ligament and tendon on fire.

All those years spent searching for pleasure
outside of myself, and now, this—
I spent hours on the boulder that day.

In the late-day light I drove home,
saw a doe bounding through a field.
For as long as I could, I stayed with her.

Graceland

When you tour Graceland with a plastic bag full of pills
in your left pocket, you will understand the irony.
You will touch them through your pants, small comfort,
waiting in line for two hours before boarding

a bus to the mansion. You'll wear a headset,
the audio kicking in when you enter
the heavy gates. An hour into the tour
you will phone the man you love and tell him

to fuck off, and then you will be alone
in Elvis's basement, looking at yourself
in the mirrored fireplace, thinking
that if Elvis were still alive you would ask

his chef to make a grilled peanut butter
and banana sandwich, and that you would watch
football on one of Elvis's three TVs.
The tour will end in the memorial garden.

Someone will kneel and say a prayer.
Someone will place a small flag on his grave.
You will make an offering as well,
taking a yellow, oval-shaped pill

from your pocket and swallowing it dry.
It will seem appropriate at the time
but, like so many things, is not.
Like so many things in life, it is not.

The Old Mill

Down 100 along the White River,
between Warren and Hancock,
through a heavy door
propped open, I'd crept inside.
I'd gone there to meet Henry Parrish,

bicycled that afternoon past
Roxbury Gap and Moss Glen Falls,
until I'd reached the old woolen mill,
whose clapboards were the color
of newsprint. The mill stood

upright despite it all, three
stories high with a cupola on top,
the heavy timber framing still
grand as I entered the main room.
The machinery sold off years ago.

But signs of life all around—
beer cans crushed, resting on their sides,
take-out containers, cigarette stubs,
evidence of a small campfire,
a circle of ash. Off the main room

sat a lone cot, the mattress swelled,
discolored, the frame sagging,
broken-legged. I'd wondered
about this place for years,
and now to be here, waiting

for Henry, dotting cherry gloss
on my lips, as the 12-over-12
windows set a hazy glow all over.
Then I heard him, finally.
Henry slipped in as I did,

had ridden his bike along the river,
past the glass blowers,
past the old Granville Inn,
closed long before we were born.
He found a push broom

and swept an area as wide
as the two of us, laid down
the wool blanket he'd brought,
and I was woozy, the late-day
light all around us, pouring

through the windows,
the dust swirl everywhere.
He pulled me close and we kissed,
his tongue a thrill in my mouth.
I clutched him, held his sides,

trembling. He took my ear in his
mouth and asked if we could 69,
but I didn't know what that meant,
so I said *can we just make love?*
Hoping that calling it that

would make it so—and he rolled
on a condom and laid me flat
and rose up on his knees.
I believed for a moment
he would make the sign

of the cross, and I thought
of my mother—how, in an instant,
I would become someone she
no longer knew. I wondered
if something cleaved in her

as it did in me—
if, at that moment in her garden,
or feeding the chickens,
she felt it, too? We moved
together, Henry and I—

I tried to keep up with him,
his knees sliding, the blanket
folding in waves against me,
the air a haze of silt, thick
with ruin—working to make

something beautiful in the old mill.
We left in a trance at twilight,
both on our bikes, a flashlight
pressed between my right palm
and the handlebar. I kept moving

until my tires found pavement,
the yellow dividing lines guiding
me home, as I pedaled away
from the old mill, the first
cathedral of my undoing.

Third Shift

He sits shotgun in the car
he'd sold to Maris for a dollar
while she drives him to the hospital.
It's springtime.
He holds a dishtowel dark with blood
between his hands.
Watching a pair of cardinals,
he'd shattered a coffee mug on the back stoop
and the pieces were sharp as hell,
he told her, and sliced his goddamn
thumb before he even knew what happened.
He doesn't do well with blood.

He works the third shift
at a warehouse, packing beauty products
into boxes. He takes his meal break
in the middle of the night—the solemnness
of men eating dinner at three a.m.,
hearing the weak sound of plastic forks
on Tupperware, then a bell, and back
to the floor until sun up.

Now he's peeling back the dishtowel,
glimpsing the damage, but she tells him
to knock it off, keep the pressure on.
Maris guesses he'll need about ten stitches
but keeps this to herself.
She wasn't far off, but he still makes
his shift, thank god, and after
a long day he drives home

from work in first light, the windows
rolled down to dilute the cologne
he'd found in a bin of discounted items,
which he'd slapped with his good hand
onto the pulse point in his neck.

For the Dog I Hit Driving Home

You were the color of a fawn.
You lived in Tunbridge, Vermont,
with a retired couple and their grandchild.
I wrapped you in a sweater and held you.

It was late summer. I'd spent the weekend
with a man who was beautiful and fleeting.
We'd picked pears from a tree in his yard.
They were small and imperfect—
we polished their rough skin on our pants.

When I knocked on your door, holding you
like an armful of cut wood, I wanted to lie
and say you were dead when I found you.
That this was someone else's doing,

and I was the one who tried to do something good—
who covered your body and brought you home.

Field Days

Last together behind his wood shed,
making out against the worn shingles
until his girlfriend tracked us down, gripping

a pitchfork as if to run us out of some
old-timey town. We'd had it coming,
ever since the county fair—we met

at the dairy show, then rubbed up against
each other in the oxen barn near those two-
thousand-pound beasts who crapped everywhere.

When his girlfriend took him back
I came straight apart. He said something
about the ability to love many people

but being morally bound to only one.
He said it so earnestly.
I told him to just die already.

He hadn't always been beautiful. Looking
through old photos I'd swiped from his top
dresser drawer, the ones before he'd figured out

how to dress, what to do with his hair—
I'd think, I'm not attracted to this man.
I would have kissed him back then

only out of sympathy.
His lack of beauty is what I cling to now.
Not us sneaking around, or the way

he'd take a block of ice in his hands and chip
off enough for our whiskeys, then kiss me
for an hour. The last time I saw him

he pulled a bobby pin out of my hair.
He wanted to run his hands straight through
my long bangs, and placed the pin

in my open palm. It was the last tender
thing he did for me. Ten minutes later
he was gone.

Ruth

My boss at the mall was cheating on his wife.
His wife's name was Ruth.
His lover took it as hers as well, and it worked

until one Ruth called right after the other—
the real one, then the fake one—
sounding nothing alike.

When he stopped hiding Fake Ruth from us,
my boss would sit with her in the back room
and they'd split a sandwich.

Her perfectly average beauty surprised me.
I was young then. Years later, when I slept
with a man who wasn't my boyfriend,

I realized it's not about the looks.
My lover was common-looking and not always kind.
Meaning, he was like my boyfriend, only new.

And Ruth, both of you, I need to tell you
what you must already know—
you were special only for a while.

How, toward the end, when either of you called
he pretended he wasn't there, rolling his eyes,
as if we were in on the joke. If you'd asked,

I couldn't have said whom I felt sorrier for.
We sigh when lovers grow old.
Then we cut them loose.

His Hand

His hand punched the fridge, an old 1950s model,
avocado green and stocky—hadn't worked for days—
the freezer dribbling its melted frost onto the floor,
the chicken breasts he'd pounded into cutlets
rotting under two inches of water.
He'd broken the first two fingers, jammed his thumb,
cracked the knuckle above his wedding band,
and with no ice around he ran the tender mess
under the sink's cool tap and wept;
the hand so badly swollen the doctor slipped a pair
of small metal snippers under the gold band and cut it off.
It was all coming apart—he made sure of that.
At home, his hand was wrapped tight, each finger
taped to the next for support—as if one broken thing
can be made whole by another.

Evidence

Polaroid photos were scattered along the curb.
It was springtime. I was young then
and on my way to school. I wore white sandals

that I'd promised to keep clean. I saw a pair
of bloody kitchen cabinets. I saw a woman
on the floor, lying on her side.

I knew I'd be in trouble for looking at her,
at the blood on the walls. But I needed
to memorize them, to remember every detail,

like the time I went to the town dump
with my father and saw a crate of dirty magazines—
one with a pretty woman on the cover,

a striped tie hanging between her bare breasts.
She was smiling. My father pulled me away.
But no one was around to stop me now.

I didn't care if I was late for school.
The fridge was beige.
The cabinets were made of knotty wood.

The floor was white with small blue squares.
Blood came out of the woman on all sides.
I don't know how I knew about death—

how I connected the blood on a scraped knee
to this. I was seeing death for the first time
and wanted to remember it. I held the proof.

The Silo Fire

It was fought in shifts, and burned for days.
Worn out, he returned at last, smelling awful—
the heavy, pungent air seeped in and stung
so badly she kicked him out of bed,
made him stand a bit longer, this time
under the force of hot water, a washcloth
and fresh bar of soap in his hands.
The deep smolder he fought for hours,
tamping out the winter's feast, burned
far from her in another world. Clean,
he came to bed again, only a hint of fire
on his being, and she knew it was over.

Snakes

Should I start with their names?
Roscoe, Willy, Big Tom, Mr. No Shoulders.
Of course I hated them,

their special tanks and lamps,
the feeding ritual. Those tongues.
The way I never felt safe.

And their sad habitat—
plastic rocks and sticks, plastic caves.
It wasn't their fault, but he—

he was the worst. One afternoon
while I was at work he took everything,
mine and his, but left his four snakes

in aquariums in the living room,
where my mother's antique table had been.
He used to pick up the snakes

and they'd wrap around his forearm.
He'd get off on it, the tightening
and squeezing, thrusting them in my face

because he knew what it did to me.
In their tanks they'd slide
over a thick piece of fake driftwood,

their scales shimmering under the heat lamp.
White mice were living in a cardboard box.
The frozen, pre-killed prey were stacked

in the freezer.
I knew how to keep everyone alive.
Did what I needed to do.

I sacrificed the mice to the snakes' hunger,
sold the snakes to a guy down the road,
and moved to a new place.

But does it make for a better story
to keep one mouse alive? To name him
Lucky, and for Lucky and me to live together?

Tenement

In a tenement shared with a dozen others,
I sleep in a closet just long enough to stretch out.
Sometimes I bring guys there.

One says he's never done it in a closet before.
Afterward he touches my hair and wraps it
around an ear. He holds me. It makes me restless,

his willingness to do something so sad.
And what of me? I'm already pregnant.
I turn the pages of a phone book with thumbs

bruised from cracking open pistachios,
dozens of them, even the ones barely open.
After it's over I come home, take the pills

to prevent infection and gag.
The undoing of an act.
A string hangs down from a light fixture

in the closet, filthy from the oils
of a thousand hands pulling it hard.
I close myself in that evening but thin light

from the hallway creeps under the door.
Should I pray for forgiveness?
I think this is how grief should look—

all hot air and shadows on the wall.
But the truth was this: I wasn't grieving.
Outside the clinic a man ate his lunch by a dumpster.

A woman brushed something off her skirt.
I'd been undoing myself for years.
Why would this day be any different?

The Story

Once, at a party, she was upright,
then not. Wasted, and hauled
to a bedroom.
Her body, folded in half,
heaved into a lofted bed.
There was a man, his pants were zipped,
then unzipped.
Her mouth was closed, then forced open.
Awake, not awake, how many ways
can that be understood?
Her pants were on, then off.
Legs closed, then not.
On her back, on her side.
Awake, not awake.
Dark in the room, then light,
the blue light of daybreak.
And her boyfriend, that night,
at another party, wondered why
she never arrived.
In the story, there's a beginning
and an end: all night captive
to the man's body,
and at sunrise, she walked home.
She had been eighteen, once.
That, too, must end.
Or not.

II.

Language of the Dream

Unseen, although she'd been here before—
tracks in the mud, in the snow,
the bobcat's den nearby.
But what did we really know?
Quick-footed, tail bobbed, ears
at attention. Some called her lynx
or catamount, they didn't know her,
though no one could call her a menace—
unlike the bold foxes darting through our yard,
or the fishers who ravaged our chickens.
She hunted rabbits, mice, voles,
until, we imagined, her muzzle turned red,
and she licked her lips clean.
How does she sleep at night, curled in her den—
a rocky outcropping, or a fallen, hollowed-out tree—
nose tucked into her paws like any other cat?
She is better than us.
She will never question her desires.
Busy at dusk and dawn, a brief union
during mating season, then apart the rest of the year.
The males alone, the females with their young.
Our girl leaves a single line of tracks—
no young, not yet.
We require so much more, don't we?
Her secrecy became an ache, her solitude an affront.
And so, what we must imagine:
under the moon, the bobcat searching for a mate,
who will be fleeting, as the last of the winter's
snow recedes from the fields.

In the diner it was so hot my thighs
stuck to the booth's plastic cushion.
Shades drawn, menus fanning
at every table, the waitstaff ready to drop.
I stared plainly at you, two booths away,
as if in a spell. Sat with my juice and one egg
scrambled, a piece of rye, and a section
of the local bi-weekly, and when you caught
me looking, I smiled with a certainty
that didn't make much sense.
You were unlike anyone I'd ever seen.
I recall what came next like a fever dream—
a wonder at your approach, your hand reaching
to touch mine, your name, your eyes,
the cash register, stacks of glassware, gallons
of cold milk, a platter of bacon passing by,
breakfast sandwiches wrapped to go,
someone setting up an extra fan
to push the hot air around a little faster.

We couldn't stop ourselves,
falling together each night, long walks
past the outskirts of town, feet raw from dancing,
beer spilled on our nice clothes.
Holding me at the waist with both hands,
you told me what seemed like everything.
Strange and alive in a park, my body
tipped back, pressed against a birch tree,
the back of my head pulled by the hair
so my mouth fell open just as your face
approached mine.
You vowed to never hurt me.
But the next night you arrived drunk at my door—
still early, still some light in the sky—
backed me into a wall, lifted my skirt
and entered me with hardly a word.
And how much I still wanted you—
not despite this, but because of it.

At the market near the falls, I buy greens
and radishes, sweet carrots for later,
samosas from the back of a truck
for right this second.
Famished after my nights with you.
Past the sandwich shop and tea house,
the medical device store, along the train tracks
all the way back home.
My neighbor, the DJ, is already rattling the walls.
I put away the food, crawl into bed,
unbutton my pants and think of you—
tender, now, after last night,
just the faintest touch, but it's enough—
the thumping bass in my chest,
my ears ringing, and you, the only thing
on my mind for weeks.
I could walk into a wall and not notice,
I could walk into traffic—
still, I would call it pleasure.

Anyone's guess where we are right now.
An old logging road, it seems, the ruts
barely visible, the grass grown in,
covered in leaves, untouched.
No compass, the sky clouded over,
the blazes lost hours ago. We're straining
for something familiar, a landmark,
a body of water, but it's just the two of us.
We've never seen each other like this,
never had to rely on one another,
although I've wanted to, lately.
Trees, brush, we look around at nothing,
struggle to hear even a bird.
We're totally fucked, aren't we, you say,
and you hold me and I stick my face
in your sweaty neck and rest my lips
on your cheek, your ear, your dark hair,
I can feel you start to rise—
you laugh and say, well, if we're going
to die out here anyway—
and for the first time, I resist you
and think clearly, and decide that, no,
we aren't going to die,
that we'll keep following the logging road,
and that we'll be OK. Somehow,
I'm going to save our lives.

We were in worse shape than I thought—
legs and arms bleeding, scratched to hell,
bug bites everywhere. Blisters, bruises
from tumbling when our legs got weak.
Lost for almost twelve hours,
we were stupid, we should have known
better. No thinking, no planning.
Just our terrible instincts.
Making it to the car, at last,
I knew we'd never be the same.
Collapsed into your apartment
with bags of cheeseburgers,
a case of beer, and devoured it all.
Marveled at our injuries,
our recklessness, touched each others'
wounds, stripped and did a tick check
and stepped into the hot shower together.
You didn't want me until I started to watch TV.
No, you said, and pulled my towel off,
and afterward, as I was lying
face down on your back,
rubbing the insoles of my feet
along the sides of your poor legs,
I told you that I loved you.

The west-running brook is low today,
quiet, like you.
You were supposed to visit last night.
The brook runs beside the field,
our field, where we once scared up
a grouse, and later, a groundhog,
a surprise around every turn.
Should I say what it's like to wait for you?
Torture, but also, a pleasure
to remember your touch, your hair,
you pressed against me
in the corner of a dark pub
near a broken popcorn machine.
Touching the wound again and again,
I must love it—your smooth stomach
on my mouth, or leaving me, once,
at three in the afternoon with a case
of Canadian beer, and what
was I supposed to do with that,
I said, it's not even my brand.
Making you over and over, here,
finding a way to keep you alive.
Days later you reappeared.
Can we try again, you asked.
And I said, of course, yes.

We dragged twin mattresses onto the floor,
fixed the wool blankets and pillows on top—
planning out all the wrong things once again—
and pulled each other down on the pile.
You left with the sky still yellow with dawn.
I'd dreamt of mountains, of hiking
and trying to grab your hand, just out of reach.
I was alone to dismantle our evening,
haul mattresses back onto frames,
fold blankets, recall your body.
I wrote a letter to you in the language of my dream—
lost in the alpine region, clouded in by storm.
(The terror of this one, wrong decision.)
To no longer see you
among delicate moss and brush,
then to lose you in low clouds.

It's the time of year when we hurt ourselves,
the landscape changing too suddenly, the once
pungent smell of manure replaced by nothing.
Stillness. Corn plowed down, gone to market,
the sad air we breathe despite ourselves.
I said goodbye to the shallow holes
where I pulled potatoes with purple skin
that fit neatly in the palm of my hand.
The black fly bite on my arm has been worried over
so much it bleeds. The cat scratches himself raw
under his chin and pulls out his fur, grabbing hold
with his mouth, tugging and tugging until it's set free.
Rising from bed I see the evidence in piles—
a wisp of grey fur sticking out of his mouth.
The decimated garden just outside the window.

I stood on the same square of linoleum
for hours, days, medicated dreams so vivid
I'd wake believing it was true, that you lived
behind the counter at the DMV
while I waited in a line twisting around
the bright room. You'd rise from under the counter,
slide your arm around another woman,
look at me and recoil. What did you think
I'd do—throw something, or scream out?
I waited so patiently. In my dreams
it was summer, but I wore a dark wool suit
and walking shoes, my cheap black heels
tucked into a briefcase, everyone else
with their bare legs, the men wearing linen shirts.
No wonder I was so uncomfortable.
No wonder the air never seemed to move,
despite the old metal fan in the corner.
Tired world. Tired dream.
I was only a dozen feet from you,
but my number is never called.
The photo machine hasn't worked for years.
I'm to return tomorrow and wait.

After sex I'd become shy, snapped back
to my true self, standing on the town green
with no clothes on, red-faced and wild-haired
and looking for my pants, while the traffic circled us.
Is this the small, sad truth about desire?
Late afternoons we watched the fields mowed down,
the aching end of summer, and opened a bottle
of something close at hand. At night my fingers
threaded the mess of hair on your chest
while you slept the blind-drunk sleep.
Bit by bit, the soft skin of your inner arm,
your heavy feet, tanned and rough—
I studied you in the weak light that showed
the outlines of things. Reckless heart.
You ask for the same things again and again.

As if I am already seeing the past—
a field of tall grass ripe for cutting,
a mower backed out of a barn,
turning towards the field that by dusk
will be shorn a few inches above the ground.
A crow picks at the insides of a squirrel
while trucks hog the road,
but he doesn't move, just stretches
his dark wings to protect his prize.
On our last night together, the deer
barely made it across the road,
its hind end lit up in our headlights.
I could hardly breathe, coming so close
with nothing to show for it. The air,
still at first, shifting in a way
I can't explain.

Nineteen days since you left.
I'd like to stand in a dark parking lot
and get clubbed with a pipe.
If I lived, I'd go to the hospital
and maybe I could finally sleep.
They'd give me ginger ale,
change my sheets every other day.
They'd pull the curtain, maybe, loosen
the ties on my gown, and bathe me in bed.
I'd close my eyes and pretend
you were here, or I was home
and you were with me,
rubbing my back before sleep.
I'd feel so lucky.
Lucky to have someone touch me,
as I imagine a nurse would now, and a physical
therapist will, later, and the doctor in a month
or two, who will start up a small saw
and crack open the cast on my arm and set me loose—
into a world where no one touches me
or folds a blanket on my lap, or shines a light
in my eyes, one at a time, asking me the year,
my hometown, when I was born.

On a sidewalk, a woman powders her face in my dreams,
wears a too-small satin robe, is lit by the light
of a streetlamp. She does her makeup
at a vanity kicked to the curb and marked
with a handwritten FREE sign.
When it begins to rain she puts on her slippers.
After smoothing her blush, she lights a smoke
and waits for the garbage collectors to come.
I'd fallen asleep again near the window,
waking to see if the woman was actually below.
And what of your dream death? My screaming your name
until I struggled for air at a rest stop in Louisiana,
I think, where I'd never been? When the trucks rolled in
to set up the flea market, I pulled maps from an old
chest of drawers, hoping they'd guide me home,
but they were all wrong—
topography maps of the Rockies, the stars in the Eastern
night sky, a map of ancient waterways. No roads.
The woman on the sidewalk was nowhere to be found,
off making herself pretty somewhere else, I suppose.
And you? Still alive. Still sleeping in another town.

I'm not beautiful like the woman in the laundromat,
who sits with a cup of coffee near the window.
At the Suds-N-Soap I drink beer and sort my clothes,
while she writes in her notebook. I stare at her,
how easily she sits with her coat on,
one hand still covered by a glove.
In a hurry, perhaps, to fix something into words.
Or cold, as I am all the time.
No, she seems to be utterly at peace,
the thin winter light resting square on her,
and outside, drifts of snow.
She knows better, she is lovely, so she must know
you can't change a man the way the snow
changes the landscape, the new dusting covering the old.
I notice everything these days,
children sliding their boots down the sidewalk,
blowing dry flakes from railings like dandelions.
The soft squares of dryer lint in the wastebasket.
The broken quarter machine with the handwritten sign—
NEED CHANGE GO TO BAR.
All of it short lived, of course. Snow, lint, things out of order.
I begin to think she has never known pain. Or love.
These days I wish for a way to cover almost all of my face.
If someone cared to see me, they'd have to look straight on.
In any case, I'd like to change. Have another drink.
No longer be the same.

III.

Storm

Agony to see them, trees coated in ice
too heavy to bear, bent to the ground
like women in gardens.
So many split in half and lie, still as air,
against one another.
Trying to get at it every night—
cursing appliances, the phone thrown
against a wall, pouring booze
into the same heavy glass
and then again.
Wouldn't it always be this way?
Sweeping glass from the floor,
then to urgent care for an X-ray,
stitches to close a gash above an eyebrow.
Try hard to recall the landscape of tall grass
and birch trees before the ice storm came.
Can you remember anything from your life?
Or—look ahead one year. Five.
So much could be resolved.
The phone placed back in its cradle.
The bourbon glaze mopped from linoleum.
Your shaking hands, after all this time, calm.

Ash

All around me
things are breaking down.
The emerald ash borer
just a few miles away,
the canopy dieback
a certainty.
Inspecting every tree
on the block won't solve
a thing anymore.
Despair overlaps despair,
branches just starting
to touch over the road,
one side stretching
toward the other.
Waking in the morning,
the darkness bears down
like a lead apron.
I bend until I give in,
letting day become night.

After You Left

Little to show of the season
beyond mud sucking at rubber boots,
faint snow still found in the shade.
Tree buds shudder in the wind,
their branches tangled or almost.

Daffodils stand in the raised bed.
Lilacs press against the air.

I kneel among the tulips you planted—
they're perfect and I cut them for myself.

The hummingbird makes a thimble-sized nest
for her eggs, passes low over short, square bushes,
catches cobwebs in her mouth.

How do the birds do it?
Welcoming, then letting go a thing
with a beating heart and mouth
and two bright eyes.

The Farmhouse

Give it new life, I thought,
the wrecked house, the apple orchard.
Camped on the edge of the property,
I'd wrapped myself in a wool blanket.
Deer hoofed through the thick field,
snapped fallen limbs
a few yards from where I slept.
Down the road lived a goat
named Festus, and when we met
I stared into his orange eyes.
His shelter was pitiful,
a small plastic dome
he ducked into when it rained.
Soon after, the house was mine.
Neighbors turned out with pies
and advice, and fresh eggs laid
by geese and bantam hens.
I tried to eat everything
before it spoiled. Cleared the brush,
peeled back layers of neglect,
while Festus stayed chained
to a metal spike in the ground,
walking in circles, wearing down
the frozen grass to bare mud.

At the Drive-In

Summer nights spent at the Weirs Beach Drive-In
in an old LeBaron convertible I'd bought for a song.
I was no longer in love.

I got some property, moved nine sheep
and a goat out of the old barn, into a truck
bound for a neighbor's farm.

Sunk an axe into infested walls, pried up
vile floorboards, saw the rubbish pile
grow a story high and burn green

when ignited, bright from years of excrement.
In quiet moments at the drive-in,
the carnival hum could be heard nearby.

Shouts and pings and cars tearing out
of parking lots. Always the smell of fried things,
or the sweat on my shirt, the skin underneath

starting to peel. I wasn't sure I could keep the property.
Couldn't hold on to anything in those days.
One night, I watched a movie at the drive-in

with a girlfriend, and at the end, when Gardner
was about to say goodbye to Debbie forever,
and they danced the fandango under the Texas

night sky, my friend was so moved she pulled
the tobacco from her lower lip, and began to cry.
And how, I thought, could I even begin to comfort her?

Backyard

The dog was so proud. I was drinking tea
on the stone steps and working on my tan.

He ran to me covered in soft fur, a small foot
hanging from the corner of his mouth.
The young rabbits had been placed in a shallow hole

by their mother. Unwise to leave things
out in the open. It's why I don't write you anymore.
The mother shouldn't have built a nest

with a dog nearby. But here, or next door,
or across the street—what's the difference?
Is it luck, then, that determines everything?

I think that's what I've been meaning to say.
I cleaned up after the dog and buried the remains
near the compost pile. I have so little to tell you.

The tea has gone cold. The dog ate four rabbits.
I can't possibly protect my heart from this world.

Starlings

I'd shoot the starlings, pick them up
by their toes and fling them to the wood's edge.
When the cats returned at night with soft feathers
around their mouths, I'd carry the menaces
deeper into the grove and bury them. Still,
the speckled riff-raff tucked into my home's
high rafters, a barn that was once theirs.
They wished it so again, visiting me in sleep
that carried me as well into the cool,
dark place beyond the tall grasses, haunted
by the living and the dead.

Practice

You must make this mistake once—
pour boiling liquid into a blender, then pulse it.
Watch the steam blow the lid straight off.
When you see your burned hands, you'll scream.
Other mistakes you repeat, finding yourself
in a familiar place, but worn out, like pigeons
circling a roof, the flock growing bigger,
then smaller. It will be this way with love.
Your neighbor plays something on the accordion,
starting and stopping before seeing it through,
but it's not what you expected. It's not even
about getting it right. You think it's about
protecting yourself, and eventually you will—
not by learning how to love, but how to do so less often.

Mercy

It was a deer, a young one. Still alive
when I stopped the car.
Its neck was broken.
I wanted to sit with the deer,
place a hand on its side.

I called the police,
then the game warden.
The warden asked, is it alive?
Yes.
Can you kill it?
What?
Do you have a gun?
No.

I searched for a big rock—to what end?
I could never do that.
I prayed it would be dead soon.
What a way to use prayer.

What I did to the deer, then could not do—

It had been grazing near heavy brush
and must have strayed from its mother.

There was no blood, no sign
of an accident, just some coarse fur caught
in my fender, like dry pine needles
sticky with sap.

Final Day

Even in August, a chill.
Boxes stacked on the painted pine floor.
Sheets pulled over the wingbacks, the sofa.
The door closed after letting in the last
of the room's good air.

Years ago I burned here.
Brought him into the near dark.
Held his hands while he breathed in my hair,
passed it between his lips.

A Wyeth print hangs on the wall now,
farmers scything the fields,
a late-summer mowing. It means
almost nothing, you know how it is,
the image passed into scenery,
or shadows, years ago.

But here, once, he held me,
his arms around my body, my arms
reflecting his own, linked to him.
It seemed that we were endless.

On this, the last night of summer,
I sleep on a cot next to an open screen
and am soaked by the night rain.

The Land

Towering brush piles, half-buried
bags of garbage, gas cans, an old motor,
a fridge, a plastic barrel of manure,

a sewing machine, endless piles of leaves,
decaying logs, mounds of soil—
god damn this place needs a new life.

On the back of the property,
a pair of pileated woodpeckers
have hollowed out a maple.

It'll be their nest, I think—
I hear them drumming nearby,
one calling to another, a loud courtship.

Working this land for months now
and still so much to reveal.
Just today, an old fire ring,

a flattened circle of smooth rocks,
a few bits of charred wood,
evidence of a gathering amid the mess.

It's all mine now, and I want to do the good,
hard work. And I want, for once,
for that to be enough.

The Owl

I'd taken the long way home,
from Ripton down to the village.
My headlights lit up
a barred owl, hunting prey.
It flew at me suddenly,
a shock of white that bent
my side mirror inward.
I'd just said goodbye to someone,
the moon not yet up, the night sky
covered in stars from end to end,
and Jupiter shining blue.
We'd taken a rambling path
through the meadow, no rush.
Desire can fade or multiply,
and I knew the kind we had.
Around us, a wall of cricket sound.
Wrapped in each others' arms so tight
I lost my breath; then we went away.
No way the poor owl had lived,
but still I pulled over, grabbed
a flashlight, and set out into the ditch,
looking for something to save.

Third Date

Can hardly joke about how bad we feel,
it's that kind of hangover.
Last night he'd cooked dinner—
it was inedible, but no matter, we ate dessert
and told all our best stories and made each other
laugh and drank everything in the house.

Outside, the mountains are quiet,
a light wind, a coyote yip, or maybe his dog
in the next room, sounding far away.
Close by, the rattle of pain reliever,
the cracking open of a sports drink.

In springtime I dream about black bears—
I run and hide but can't lose them,
and wake exhausted, vowing to never
enter the woods again. He isn't scared
of wild animals like I am; already, he's
promised to keep me whole. Back in bed,
I press myself into the small of his back,
trace my fingernails in looping arcs.

He pulls me close, buries his head
against me, my heart racing as it does
when I drink too much. His stubble scrapes me
and we decide there's only one true way
to forget the pain for a moment, and slowly,
through waves of nausea and head drumming,
we begin to make what I think is love.

The Forester

We talk of shit—
the coyote's, smack in the middle of the trail.
Or moose droppings, discovered after his dog
rolled in a pile, ecstatic.
I thought we were mostly safe.

But he points to loose limbs caught
in the crown of a tree
and calls them widow makers.
Shows me, too, the deadly tension
of spring poles—young saplings, bent over.

In the forestry service,
these details kept him alive.
But on a casual stroll in the woods,
it's alarming. We pass a red maple
and I say its Latin name,

acer rubrum, the only one I recall.
He knows the rest, and recites them
as their ancient names hang in the air.
Once, on the shore of a mountain lake
after a swim, he found a leech on the back

of my leg, and calmly slid a fingernail
under the sucker and tossed it away.
At first I thought he might know too much,
had seen too much, to enjoy the woods,
but it's not that—

to hear him talk about tree diseases,
the blights and bleeding cankers,
molds, rots, and fungi, the strange poetry
of *declines* and *diebacks*—
it's the chance of harm amid such beauty.

What we can manage, and what is beyond us.
One night over drinks, he told me a story
from years of fighting wildfires out West—
as his crew set up a fire break, a rabbit bolted
from the flames, burning alive, seconds from death.

Someone laughed. Others pretended
they didn't notice. All these years later,
one of the saddest things he'd ever seen.
I'm not sure how to explain it, he told me.
It was just a rabbit, he said. But it was on fire.

The Wedding

The man I once loved, whom I'd been hiding from
all night, found me and led me away from the white tent

and into the steady rain to show me his new life.
The grass had become a mess of mud.

He walked me to his car where his wife sat,
nursing their new son. They were tired from travel,

but happy. I couldn't help it—I started to cry.
I tried to leave but my car was stuck in the mud.

My shoes were ruined. I took some cardboard
from my trunk and placed it in front of the rutted-down tire,

and tried again. But I wasn't moving.
I had a bottle of wine in the car, and drank almost all of it.

I listened to music coming from the tent
and heard laughter and applause.

By the time the rain stopped it was almost dusk.
The wrecked fields misted up toward the pink sky.

The Accident

Why hadn't I noticed it before,
the protrusion below his shoulder?
My fingers press into the nub,

move up and down over the raised bone,
my palm grazing the spot above his heart.
His collarbone had given way long ago

after a drunken night in the valley,
when he'd pedaled his bike into a parked car.
We'd been together for a while,

but this was new to me.
The bone had taken three months to heal.
He'd slept propped up, immobilized

on a recliner in his parents' television room,
sweating out the summer.
His mother had sliced strips of stick deodorant

with a worn-out knife, and carefully pressed them
into the ripe space between arm and body,
into the dampness of skin and hair.

I know his body, know what it does to mine,
and in his small bed my fingers grasp
this bit of helplessness.

He told me how, after the accident,
he'd wake in the night delirious
from the pain and drugs,

and sense he'd been babbling, crying.
Could still feel his mouth moving,
could taste the words still wild on his lips.

Love Poem

He sleeps so soundly I can play music
a few inches from his head, and still, nothing.
Sleeps through the night storm, the thunder
shaking the old windows I'll never replace,
the ones with broken sash pins.
I gather the clumps of tissues on his side and mine,
take them to the bathroom where I clean up,
find my clothes where we'd left them.
Lights on next door at Maxine's, her baby up again,
his wail in waves from behind the line of cedars.
The woodworker across the street had a busy day,
carving giant bears out of stumps,
then an eagle, then the face of a dog.
The carvings stand watch
and I pose unclothed before them,
framed by a window, covered in darkness,
a bit of moonlight shining through.
No risk of being seen, only the tender thrill of this life—
walking the hall nude; a home and neighbors;
this man, sleep-breathing in my bedroom,
who, if I'll let him, might just stay for good.

Summer

A young woman was pleasuring herself
on a pine tree that had fallen across
the narrow river where I went to fish,
straddling the trunk, her feet just breaking
the water, her body leaning forward
with hands pressed into the bark.
White shorts rode up her thighs and bunched
at her crotch as she settled into an uneven rhythm.

I thought of love, and you, my love.
But here, now, I see it—watching her ride the tree,
lifting one hand and then the other to wave
at the sky like a conductor, this quiet expression of pleasure,
this face of surprise. Strange angel—
no matter how much she rocked herself
she would not loosen the tree from its resting place,
she would not set forth down the river,
drifting somewhere new, somewhere east of here.

Notes

Epigraph: Four lines from "In the Lupanar at Pompeii" from *The Whole Motion: Collected Poems 1945-1992* © 1994 by James Dickey. Published by Wesleyan University Press. Used by permission.

"The Old Mill" is after James Dickey's "Cherrylog Road."

"Language of the Dream" owes a debt to "The School of Dreams" by Hélène Cixous, "Book of Dog" by Cleopatra Mathis, and "Twenty-One Love Poems" by Adrienne Rich.

ACKNOWLEDGMENTS

Grateful acknowledgment is made to the following publications where these poems first appeared:

Amsterdam Review: "The Accident," "The Farmhouse," and "Final Day"

B O D Y: "Summer"

The Collagist: "His Hand" and "Practice"

The Cortland Review: "Backyard"

District Lit: "After You Left"

Guernica: "Tenement"

The Indianapolis Review: "The Owl"

New England Review: "Ritual" and "Graceland"

Ninth Letter: "At the Drive-In"

On the Seawall: "The Old Mill" and "Field Days"

Split Rock Review: "The Forester"

Stonecoast Review: "Third Shift"

Enormous thanks to Gary Soto for selecting my manuscript for the Barry Spacks Poetry Prize and to David Starkey and Chryss Yost at Gunpowder Press for their hard work and support in bringing this book to life.

Thank you to Wyn Cooper for his great eye, good humor, and support.

Thank you to the Bread Loaf School of English, the Bread Loaf Writers' Conferences, the Warren Wilson MFA Program for Writers, the Larry Levis Post-Graduate Stipend, the Vermont Arts Council Creation Grant, the Vermont Studio Center, and The Grind for being such extraordinary sources of community, learning, and support for writers.

Thank you to Middlebury College for the gift of the Continuing Education Fund that supported my graduate work over the years.

Thank you to my teachers: Debra Allbery, James Allen, David Baker, Jennifer Grotz, Jane Hirshfield, David Huddle, Randy Pfeiffer, Carl Phillips, Martha Rhodes, Alan Shapiro, Tom Sleigh, Ann Townsend, and C. Dale Young.

To my friends in life and writing from Ohio, Squam, and Vermont, with special thanks to Elizabeth Ellis Barrentine, Noreen Cargill, Alex Cudaback, Denise Delgado, Johanna Derlega, Christian Gullette, Maggie Hogan, Kerry and Sam Jackson, Brandon Kooman, Jason Lamb, Jason Lersch, Carrie Macfarlane, Matthew Müller, Matthew Nienow, Matthew Olzmann, Becky Roberts, Robert Sullivan, Karen Tucker, Laura Van Prooyen, and Ross White.

Thank you to the Middlebury College Libraries for being an extraordinary resource and to my terrific colleagues who make it all possible.

To all the caregivers and teachers of young children in Middlebury who have given my family so much support over the years.

To the Hendrickson family, especially Richard and Wendy Hendrickson, for their love and encouragement.

To all my dear aunts, uncles, and cousins for their love and hilarity.

To my brother and sister-in-law, Bennett and Katie Ayres, for being the very best.

To my amazing parents, Tom and Ann Ayres, for a lifetime of love, support, and friendship.

And to Corey Hendrickson, and Fielding and Sawyer—my dearest loves, my heart—thank you.

About the Poet

Kellam Ayres's poems have appeared or are forthcoming in *New England Review*, *Ploughshares*, *Guernica*, and elsewhere. She received a Vermont Arts Council Creation Grant and is a graduate of the Warren Wilson MFA Program for Writers and the Bread Loaf School of English. She works for the Middlebury College Library and lives with her family in Vermont.

BARRY SPACKS POETRY PRIZE

2023
In the Cathedral of My Undoing, by Kellam Ayres
selected by Gary Soto

2022
Accidental Garden, by Catherine Esposito Prescott
selected by Danusha Laméris

2021
Like All Light, by Todd Copeland
selected by Lynne Thompson

2020
Curriculum, by Meghan Dunn
selected by Jessica Jacobs

2019
Drinking with O'Hara, by Glenn Freeman
selected by Stephen Dunn

2018
The Ghosts of Lost Animals, by Michelle Bonczek Evory
selected by Lee Herrick

2017
Posthumous Noon, by Aaron Baker
selected by Jane Hirshfield

2016
Burning Down Disneyland, by Kurt Olsson
selected by Thomas Lux

2015
Instead of Sadness, by Catherine Abbey Hodges
selected by Dan Gerber

ALSO FROM GUNPOWDER PRESS

Before Traveling to Alabama, poems by David Case
Mother Lode, poems by Peg Quinn
Raft of Days, poems by Catherine Abbey Hodges
Unfinished City, poems by Nan Cohen
Original Face, poems by Jim Peterson
Shaping Water, poems by Barry Spacks
The Tarnation of Faust, poems by David Case
Mouth & Fruit, poems by Chryss Yost

CALIFORNIA POETS SERIES
Downtime, poems by Gary Soto
Speech Crush, poems by Sandra McPherson
Our Music, poems by Dennis Schmitz
Gatherer's Alphabet, poems by Susan Kelly-DeWitt

ALTA CALIFORNIA CHAPBOOKS
EMMA TRELLES, SERIES EDITOR
On Display, poems by Gabriel Ibarra (selected by Francisco Aragón)
Sor Juana, poems by Florencia Milito (selected by Francisco Aragón)
Levitations, poems by Nicholas Reiner
Grief Logic, poems by Crystal AC Salas